Mom,
You're So Annoying!

by

Michelle Weinberger

DORRANCE
PUBLISHING CO
EST. 1920
PITTSBURGH, PENNSYLVANIA 15238

Dorrance Publishing Co
585 Alpha Drive
Pittsburgh, PA 15238
Visit our website at *www.dorrancebookstore.com*

ISBN: 978-1-4809-4239-4
eISBN: 978-1-4809-4262-2

Dedicated to my kids,
Gabrielle and Derek,
and to all the parents,
especially the moms

Mom,
You're So Annoying!

Spoken by a true adolescent
Parenting from puberty to the empty nest
My kids, your kids

Introduction

No matter what you say or don't say, no matter how young, how old, no matter if you say enough of it or not enough! In other words, no matter what, you are going to be told that you are being annoying . . . It's funny how this comment is said by kids of all ages to all parents. They swear by it and mean it when they say it!

Being a mom is like a comedy show at times. The conversations, the remarks, the sayings and the sarcasm, etc., etc. But it comes with the territory.

Parenting is one of life's greatest joys—and greatest challenges. From the first moment of holding a newborn baby in your arms, having children absolutely changes your life. This new life is your responsibility: not only to keep safe and healthy, but to teach the child right from wrong, good from bad, and to give him or her everything needed to grow into a happy and successful person.

Then the child gets old enough to talk—and talk back. Before very long, this child who depended on you for everything, and looked up to you in wonder and amazement, is rewarding you for your concern and your good intentions by rolling their eyes and saying, "Mom, you're so annoying!"

For many parents, the irony of hearing such a thing from their child can be tough to take. Here you are, wanting the best for your children and seeking to teach them the right way of doing something, patiently explaining how to fold laundry or look both ways before crossing the street, and you find all your tender concern met with a remark like "Mom, you've already said that a hundred times!"

What else can a parent do but laugh? With any luck, you'll get to watch your children grow up to be happy, well-adjusted adults with kids of their own—kids who will freely tell your adult children how annoying they are. It may be only then that your children truly appreciate what they put you through, and that when you asked them four times if they were *sure* they didn't want to bring a jacket or pack a snack, you had only their best interests at heart, and your worry and concern for them.

Until that time, *Mom, You're So Annoying!* exists to let parents know that they're not alone. Whether you've heard your son or daughter say the words "Mom, you're so annoying!" or perhaps merely watched your children roll their eyes at you, the book you hold in your hands presents observations and anecdotes from every part of parenting, with situations every parent can relate to.

From serving as a chauffeur to your children and driving them from school to sports and other after-school activities, to acting as a detective, finding lost items and investigating your children's alibis, and from playing the role of "Dr. Mom," diagnosing and treating a range of illnesses, to calling upon your super powers as "Super Mom," able to find lost homework and whip up cookies for the school bake sale at the last minute, *Mom, You're So Annoying!* offers a wide range of experiences that parents can identify with and laugh about.

While parenting truly is one of life's greatest joys, the day-to-day frustration, the sacrifices, your time, money, and sanity for the happiness and health of your children can be exhausting. This book offers you the reassurance that you're not alone, and will help you laugh in recognition of the many roles you play, and the unconditional love and support you offer your children . . . only to be rewarded by being told how annoying you are!

Chapter One

Teacher/School

One of the key responsibilities for any parent is to make sure your child is learning. You may say that that's the role of the school. Children are learning all the time, in and out of school. Add to those basic skills like talking, walking, and reading, and every child has learned quite a lot from his or her parents, well before they first venture inside a school!

And on top of that, the child's formal education is considered the responsibility of the parent. Who gets called in when a child misbehaves? Who is asked to sign a report card?

And don't forget about the parent's job as on-the-spot tutor, homework checker, and project helper. It doesn't matter if math was never your best subject: it's your job to look over your child's shoulder and make sure all the right answers are in the right place. And when your child has to stay up late making a diorama of the solar system, guess who else will be staying up late, holding the rings of Saturn steady while the child glues them into place?

When you consider the wide range of duties the parent takes on as soon as the child goes off to school, it's plain to see that "Teacher" is another of the hats every parent must wear at some time or another.

But as with most of the roles a parent must take on, part of the parent's challenge is to face the sting of the child's reaction simply for doing the right thing.

Here is a case in point:

When my son was a young boy in elementary school, there were a number of occasions when I was called upon to get involved in his education—not as a tutor or field-trip chaperone, unfortunately, but because he had gotten into some kind of trouble.

Whether he had been sent to the principal or given detention, I would try to take the opportunity to make sure my son had learned something from the situation. If my son had pushed another boy for taking his toy, I would say, "You can't go around pushing people. Instead of pushing this boy, you should have asked him to please give you back your toy. If that didn't work, you could go to the teacher and let her know what happened."

Whenever I told my son something like this, I finished by saying, "These are the rules. There's a right way to do something and a wrong way. I want you to do things the right way always."

My son would automatically respond by telling me that not only was the principal or teacher involved wrong, and stupid, but *I* was wrong, too.

Not only that, but by scolding him I was showing that I was on *their* side instead of *his* side! "You always stick up for them," he would say. "You never stick up for me."

Of course, if I tried to re-state my point that I was trying to teach him to do the right thing and not the wrong thing, that there were rules and systems you have to live by if you want things to run smoothly, he would just get annoyed all over again. He knew he was right, and everyone who was against him was wrong—teachers, principals, deans, other students, and now *me*.

Often, this would be the time that I would hear that classic line, "Mom, you're so annoying!"

I thought, "Wow, how could I be so annoying?"

But of course, part of the parent's duty is to not waver in the face of your child's disapproval. As parents, we remained absolutely firm that there is a right way to do something, and a wrong way, and we would never accept the wrong way from our children—no matter how annoying that made us!

Chapter Two

Supermom

If your family is anything like mine, Mom is the one who makes it all happen. Whether it's cooking a nutritious meal, dropping the kids off, or making sure they've done their homework, Mom is at the center of it all.

But her job responsibilities go way beyond these fairly ordinary tasks. It's not enough for moms to take on the daily tasks of running a household and raising children. She's also called upon to be **Supermom**!

Who is Supermom, you ask? She's the one who finds that pair of lost sneakers and drives them to school in time for her child's gym class, so that he or she doesn't lose any points for being unprepared.

She's the one who finds out about the school bake sale just an hour or so before the event—and yet still manages to whip up a couple dozen delicious brownies and cookies.

In other words, Supermom is the one who does the impossible, springing into action in a matter of seconds, in just the snap of a finger, to help her children. Whether it's sewing a Halloween costume just minutes before the child goes out trick-or-treating, staying up half the night working on a school project, or cooking a new meal from scratch to suit a picky eater, Mom is truly a superhero—Supermom!

Like a true superhero, Supermom does all these incredible feats not for attention or acclaim, but to make her children's lives easier: to make sure they get good grades, to keep them warm and fed, and perhaps most of all, to make them happy. Sure, some recognition—a warm "Thank you"—would be wonderful, but Supermom is motivated by a desire to care for her children and give them the best.

Of course, part of Supermom's role as a child-rearing superhero is to develop good habits in her kids, teaching them the right values to succeed in school and well beyond. It's only natural, after another crisis has occurred with a forgotten lunch, a dry-cleaned costume for the school play, or a poster completed for class with just seconds to spare. Supermom wants to teach her children how to avoid such situations in the future.

"This is not the first time you've done this," Supermom might say to her child. "How can you avoid getting into this situation the next time?"

Supermom isn't trying to make her children feel bad, but is only encouraging them to be more conscientious in the future, taking responsibility for their work and themselves.

That's why it can irritate even Supermom, after another heroic effort, achieving success against impossible odds, to watch her child turn to her with a frown and to hear those words that strike such a chord in her heart: "Mom, you always say that! You're so annoying!"

But as all moms out there know, one of Supermom's greatest strengths is her thick skin. And so despite her child finding her annoying, or telling her that she's repeating herself, the next time that child needs a rip in their clothes patched before the bus arrives, or a permission slip signed and returned in the next half-hour, you can depend upon Supermom to rise to the occasion and save the day, no matter how long the odds may be.

One story from my daughter's school days will prove beyond a doubt that a parent will do anything she has to in order to help her kids.

One day I was taking a shower when I heard the phone ringing. I got out of the shower, toweled off quickly, and put on my bathrobe. When I answered the phone, it was my daughter. She'd forgotten her homework and needed me to bring it to her at school immediately. She sounded frantic.

Without another thought, I ran and grabbed her homework where she'd left it on her desk. I rushed out to the car, started the engine, and drove off toward the school. I was going so fast, and in my haste to get there and give my daughter her homework I went through a stop sign. Before I knew it, a police officer was behind me, the lights of his car flashing and the siren blaring.

My first thought was not that I was in trouble, or that I was going to get a ticket. It was that my daughter needed her homework immediately and this BETTER not take too long!

When the police officer came up to my window, he seemed surprised to see that the driver of the car he'd pulled over was dressed only in a bathrobe. I was in such a rush, I hadn't bothered to get dressed!

"Officer, my daughter called me and she needs this homework right away," I told him. "I'm sorry about the stop sign, but can you let me go this time so I can take this to her?" I even told him that he should follow me to the school and give me the ticket there so I could get this homework to my daughter.

He didn't know what to say. For a second or two he just looked at me like I was out of my mind, as if he didn't believe what he was hearing! Then he said, "**I'm afraid I can't do that, ma'am**."

I still didn't care what he said. I was still thinking of driving off, leaving him there and continuing to the school, when my cell phone rang. "Excuse me, officer," I said. "It's my daughter."

When I picked up, my daughter's voice was far calmer than when she'd called before, frantic about her missing homework. "Mom, it turns out I don't need the homework now after all," she said. "I can just turn it in tomorrow."

"Oh, okay, honey," I said, knowing that my daughter had no idea whatsoever of where I was calling from: pulled over, standing beside a police officer, dressed only in a bathrobe.

After my daughter and I hung up, I explained to the police officer what had happened, giving him a smile. He did not smile back. I got a ticket for running the stop sign.

My husband was not very happy with me when he found out what had happened, but I have to admit I would do the same thing if that situation happened today. A mom will do anything she has to to help her kids. She will do anything and everything that will help her kids, improve their lives, or save them from getting in trouble. True, sometimes it might be good for kids to get into trouble and face the consequences of their actions (or lack of action), just so that they can learn and try to avoid making those same mistakes in the future. But Supermom can't help doing anything she has to to help her kids.

It's all in a day's work for Supermom.

Chapter Three

Social Life and Friends

One of the toughest adjustments for any parent to make is when their children start to have lives outside of the house. It's an important part of growing up! Making friends at school, meeting for play dates, going to a friend's home for a birthday party, taking your children and their friends to the movies, or even going to a friend's for a sleepover can be very nerve-wracking. The responsibility of driving your child all over and their friends is a big responsibility, even stressful, but most parents are happy to see their children making friends, having fun, and beginning to develop into their own people.

All that changes though, when your children get a little older. It's one thing to be a chauffeur and take your child to a friend's house where parents will watch over them, and where you yourself may even be invited to stay. By the time your child reaches the teenage years, however, the last thing he or she wants is for one of his parents to tag along, bowling in the next lane or reaching over for a handful of their popcorn at a movie. Even the slightest suggestion that you might come in to say hello to a friend's parents is likely to be enough to hear that classic line "Mom, you're so annoying! You're the only parent that does this!"

Pretty soon, most parents are remembering with fond memories the days when the most worrisome part of their kids' social lives was making sure they brought an appropriate present to the party or being on time to pick them up. As children grow older, they develop lives of their own, and they don't want their parents to know everything they do. It's a natural development . . . unfortunately, it goes against the parent's natural inclination to want to know *everything* their child is doing, from *who* they are hanging out with and *where* they are going, to *when* they will be home and *why* they are dressed that way. The more a parent pushes, overloading the child with questions and instructions—be home by ten o'clock, don't talk to strangers, look both ways before you cross the street!—the less the child wants to give them any answers. (And the more the parent is likely to hear about how annoying they are being!)

The moment when your child begins to break away, building their independence by going out with friends and making their own plans, seems to come all at once, an overnight change that makes it feel like the child went to bed an innocent, adorable toddler and woke up an independent teenager with a bad attitude and a mind of their own. For many parents, there's a strong urge to teach the child everything they'll need to know out there, overloading them with advice and tips on how to avoid danger.

"Don't talk to strangers!" you might tell the child. "Don't take a ride from someone you don't know!"

The advice comes from a good place. After all, parents just want what is best for their children. To the child, though, it seems all this good-intentioned advice and wisdom can't help but be irritating—a lot of obvious tips that seem to say to the child, "I still think you're a baby" and "I don't trust you to make your own decisions." Like many situations growing up, your kids may not fully understand your point of view until they're parents themselves.

Until then, you can expect to hear *their* point of view loud and clear: "Stop repeating yourself! You've said that a hundred times!" And of course: "Mom, you're so annoying!"

Chapter Four

Chauffeur

Every mother and father wants to see their child active and engaged, making friends and living an active life of sports, sleepovers, and parties. We would worry about our children if all they wanted to do was stay inside, watching television by themselves, never going to a friend's birthday party, never begging to go to the mall or to the movies.

But as the people responsible for taking the children to those baseball games, play dates, and parties, and picking them up again after it's all over, you can't blame parents for sometimes thinking, "I wish my kid would just stay home once in a while."

Unfortunately, that's highly unlikely. Which is why one of the biggest roles a parent must take on, and one that requires quite a bit of time, stress, aggravation, and rushing on the parent's part. That is the *chauffeur*. From morning to night, the parent can feel like little more than a paid driver, forced to provide the child with door-to-door service, braving traffic and bad weather and looking up directions to the most obscure locations while your child sits in the back seat, lost in video games or a cell phone, ignoring you except to occasionally ask, "Are we there yet? How many more minutes?"

And all this, mind you, without any of the benefits of being an actual chauffeur—such as being paid.

Of course, that's just your child's social schedule. Who could forget the biggest part of the chauffeur's duties, getting their child to school on time?

For most parents, this is another situation where the job of an actual chauffeur must sometimes seem easy, even preferable to the job of a parent—after all, all the chauffeur has to do is drive. As the parent-chauffeur, we get the luxury of waking cranky children, nagging them to hurry up and get dressed, and putting breakfast on the table.

Naturally, if the child is late to school and ends up getting in trouble, it doesn't make a bit of difference to the child that he slept an extra fifteen minutes after you first woke him up, or that she had to try on four different outfits before she was satisfied. Who gets the blame when the child is late? You guessed it—the chauffeur, of course!

Another duty that parents face, that can make the job of being a professional chauffeur look downright appealing, is the need to feed kids while on the go. After all, most rich people who hire chauffeurs don't expect their hired drivers to also prepare and deliver meals. Yet that's what many children are accustomed to. If you forget to pack them a snack or you're a little late in getting them lunch, you'll certainly hear about it!

In today's super-busy world, kids are scheduled from dawn to dusk, and the "chauffeur"—better known as Mom—has to take them from school to the practice field or any after-school activity, then out to the store for clothing or school supplies. Eating in the car has, sadly, become a necessity.

Despite the best-laid plans, however, it's inevitable that there will be spills, stains, and pieces of food wedged between your seats and ground into your car mats. It's just the price you pay when you are a chauffeur who's also a restaurant on wheels.

Of course, even driving *and* feeding your children is not the end of the parent-chauffeur's job duties. Just as it is up to you to get your children to school on time, the responsibility also falls to you to make sure they get their homework done. Considering the amount of time kids today spend in the car, going from one activity or event to another, there's no escaping it: at some point, you are going to have to help your child with his or her homework while you're stuck in traffic, hurtling along a highway at seventy miles an hour, or trying to listen to the directions on your GPS.

It's a lot to throw at a chauffeur—but of course, you are much more than a mere chauffeur. As a driver/tutor, you can expect to be asked to recall everything you know about the Battle of Gettysburg, long division, and *MacBeth* while you drive the child from school to soccer practice. The level of distraction involved in trying to explain a math problem your child doesn't understand could well make texting and driving look easy! LOL.

As if all that weren't enough, there's one more hat the chauffeur-parent must wear (and it's not one of those cool driving caps that actual chauffeurs get to wear). It's the "referee" hat. As in those guys in the black and white striped shirts you see in the boxing ring. Because once you get on the road—and especially if you're on a long car ride—it's just inevitable that there are going to be fights in the back seat.

Someone touching the other person's side of the seat, making faces, refusing to share snacks or games or books, even farting—anything can be the cause of a conflict that could soon spiral into verbal screaming, hitting, punching, and kicking. As the parent-chauffeur-cook-referee, it's up to you to intervene.

Unfortunately, your options are limited. There's the stern warning—for example, "Don't make me turn this car around." There's the technique of reaching back to break it up, swatting at one or both children. Your kids are probably smart enough to know that you're not *actually* going to turn the car around and go back home. Your strongest option is most likely going to be pulling the car over, turning to face the back seat dramatically, and yelling at your kids to cut it out. It may not seem like much, but in the confined space of a car, it's all you can do. And for better or worse, it's also the most powerful weapon at your command . . . until you get home.

No matter how many hats you end up wearing, one thing you can depend on is that your kids are not going to appreciate all you are doing to help them get from one place to another, on time, with their bellies full, their homework done, and their bodies not (too) sore or bruised from fighting with their siblings.

In fact, if you point out to them how much you are doing for them, the self-sacrifice, the devotion, and that they can at least make things easier for you, it still doesn't matter. You will still hear the familiar comment: "Mom, you're so annoying!"

Unlike a real chauffeur, you're almost definitely not getting a tip!

Chapter Five

Halloween

Halloween can be a scary time of year for a parent—and not because of all the witches, ghosts, and horror-movie characters wandering around the neighborhood. Halloween is a time when the parent must let his or her child out into the world, encountering strangers and asking for sugary treats. For a mother who takes care of her child's every need and want, letting the child loose to walk around in the dark can be a very spooky occasion.

It's yet one more time when a parent must learn to give the child a bit of independence, trusting that everything the child has learned about dealing with strangers, looking both ways when crossing the street, and saying "Please" and "Thank you" will kick in. Of course, in the weeks and days leading up to the big night, it can be tempting for the parent to "remind" the child of these good habits, sometimes going a little too far in stressing different behaviors, and hearing the swift response of "Mom, you already said that a hundred times!"

Halloween can also be bittersweet for parents who have fond memories of dressing their child at a young age and walking the neighborhood with the child holding their hand tight, too nervous to walk up a stranger's steps alone, much less vanish from their mother's sight. It can be a bit sad to realize that that child no longer wants to be seen walking around the neighborhood with his or her mother, much less holding hands. And for nervous parents, glancing at their watches and wondering how much later their child will be trick-or-treating is sure to bring back memories of the days when their children were back home before dark, exhausted after a trip up and down the block.

Of course, the parental struggles and worries that go along with Halloween start long before the night itself. A parent may start planning weeks or months in advance, asking the child what he or she would like to dress up as this year. It's only reasonable for a parent to want some time to help the child prepare the costume, possibly scouring nearby stores for masks, items of clothing, or even bolts of fabric with which to create the desired costume. Be careful, however—ask once or twice too often about the costume your child is thinking about, and you're liable to be told that you're nagging your child, asking the same thing over and over again.

When it comes to making the costume, applying the right make-up to turn your child into a ghoul or a princess, and all the other work that goes into preparing your child for Halloween, it's taken for granted that it will all just get done. How? They don't think of it!

Even after a costume has been chosen, and either bought or created, there is still quite a lot for a mother to worry about. There are rules for trick or treating, as well as "do's" and "don'ts" that parents hope their children will follow on the big night. As a parent, you hope that your child will be polite when asking strangers for candy, using words like "please" and "thank you" instead of "gimme" and "more!" Especially if you live in a neighborhood where everyone tends to know everyone else, your kids represent you when they go out there, and a plastic mask or some ghoulish make-up won't be enough to disguise the fact that your child just grabbed three handfuls of Snickers bars from the house up the street.

Mostly, though, a parent's worries center on the dangers of the unknown. When a mother sees her son or daughter head out of sight with the sun setting, it doesn't take long before her imagination begins to run wild. What if someone doesn't see my son, dressed all in black as the Grim Reaper, as he crosses the street? What if my daughter's cheerleader outfit is too skimpy, and she catches a bad cold?

Most parents probably have a pretty good idea of what will happen, though, if they suggest that their son wear a reflective vest over their Grim Reaper costume, or put on a light jacket over that cheerleading outfit—"Mom, there's nothing scary about Death if he's got a reflective vest on" or "Cheerleaders don't wear jackets!" or, simply, "Mom, you're ruining Halloween!"

But a parent's most vivid and frightening worries are reserved for a very different kind of danger: sick, bad people trying to harm their precious children. There's no escaping the stories: a candied apple that turns out to have razor blades in it, or a Snickers bar full of needles or broken glass. Forget witches and ghosts—*these* are the scariest parts of Halloween, at least where parents are concerned.

In recent years, some hospitals have offered free candy-screening services, sending children's bags through the X-ray machine to look for nasty surprises. Even if you don't go that far as a parent, it's still your duty to inspect your child's haul, looking for suspiciously open wrappers or "weird" items like cookies in Ziploc bags, popcorn balls, or fruit. In most cases, your kids will thank you for getting rid of any fruit they may have received. They'll be less understanding, though, if they see you toss out a full-sized bag of M&Ms. Patiently explaining that the bag is ripped and there's a chance that some lunatic may have slipped pins, poison, drugs, or worse in with all the delicious candy—that won't do much to change your child's mind, unfortunately. The mother who wants to protect her child is going to have to be ready to hear things like "That's *my* candy!" and "You're ruining Halloween!" and even that old classic.

Even when the child is back home, safe and sound, and you've sorted through your child's candy looking for suspicious items, your job is not quite over. While razor blades and poison may be the greatest danger to your child's health, there's another danger you must guard against—the sugar rush. (This can also be a danger to your own patience and sanity.)

That's right: now that your child has spent several hours walking the streets, gathering this hard-earned candy, it is your job to step in and lay down some rules about how much candy the child can have right now. Some parents have strict rules in place—just one or two pieces now—while others are more lenient. But no parent in his or her right mind wants to deal with a child who is bouncing off the walls until 3 A.M., to say nothing of the dentist's bills down the road. It can feel a little like going into a lion's cage, but a mother's duty now is to step forward and dole out the appropriate amount of candy, then put the rest of the candy away, saving it for another day.

Unfortunately for parents, a child with an enormous pile of candy resting in front of him or her is usually not very understanding about having that candy confiscated. Expect some tears, and maybe even a tug-of-war, with the bag of candy in the middle. At the very least, you can expect to hear your child say some pretty angry and emotional things. "That's *my* candy!" is something you might hear, along with "You ruin everything!" or "I hate Halloween!" And of course, there's always that classic line.

Chapter Six

Judge

As much as parents may try to teach their children right from wrong, and establish sensible rules that everyone can follow, the truth about parenting is that kids are going to fight. It's inevitable and expected!

It's just the nature of children to misbehave, whether it's by mistake, boredom, testing boundaries, or just because they're children. While there are many different ways kids can act up and break the rules, for a parent the really important thing is that once your child has misbehaved, how do you, as an authority figure, respond appropriately?

That means not just being the cop who catches them in the act, but the judge who handles the matter in a fair, even-handed way. That means listening to their side of the story and the other side of the story and coming up with a reasonable solution. One that fits the crime and gives the child something to think about next time.

If there is anything that *Mom, You're So Annoying!* should teach parents out there, it's that being a good parent means wearing many different hats. In this case, it also means wearing a robe—the black robe worn by the judge.

One thing that's certain—your judgments are not going to be very popular with your kids! Even wise King Solomon, handing down his pronouncements on cases, could not have avoided hearing complaints like "That's not fair!" or "You never take my side!"—especially if he ever had to make decisions about his own children.

Of course, "criminal court" in the home is just one side of the story. In addition to handing out appropriate punishments to children who misbehave, the mother of multiple children will often find herself taking on another side of the judge's role: hearing complaints and ruling in favor of one child against the other. It can be very complicated. LOL!

Just like when you had to decide upon a punishment for your child, in cases of disputes your children will be paying close attention to the decisions you make on who started a fight, whose turn it is to wash the dishes, or any of a thousand other small and tricky disputes that may arise. You will be astonished by the careful attention to detail shown by a son or daughter who ordinarily cannot be bothered to notice.

Just as in the case of "criminal" cases within the home, there is much for Judge Mom to think about. Working hard not to show favoritism, setting and following rules, and giving the child "something to think about" the next time he or she is in a similar situation, all are considerations Judge Mom must weigh when making a decision.

Just as important, however, is the parent's key duty, one that has come up time and time again throughout this book: teaching children the difference between right and wrong. A wise judge knows that settling a dispute over one child ripping up a sibling's homework is not just about the present moment, but about leaving both children with a lasting lesson in determining right from wrong and trying, always, to do the right thing.

Of course, as with so many lessons in this book, the judge's true wisdom may not be appreciated for years, even decades, to come—not until these children who are now facing Judge Mom's decision find themselves wearing the black robe and making a decision on their own children's behavior.

Until that time, a sincere and well-meaning parent can expect their decisions to be met with jeers and cries of disbelief from plaintiffs and defendant alike: "You never listen to me!" and "This is so unfair!" along with "You always blame me!" And of course, that old complaint, "Mom, you're so annoying!"

Chapter Seven

A Parent's Role as Doctor

One of the many roles every parent has to play is that of doctor. A child's health and well-being are your responsibility, and naturally you want only the best for your child.

When your son or daughter looks ill, can't talk, is burning up, or suddenly comes down with an ear-piercing, barking cough, of course any mother will be concerned and will jump into action in their role as on-the-spot doctor . . .

. . . Only to be rewarded, after asking one too many questions about where it hurts, pressing a hand to the child's forehead, or trying to take a temperature, with the classic remark, "Mom, you're so annoying!"

It never fails.

This is true even in cases where the child comes to you, saying, "Mom, I don't feel well." Although you, as a parent, may not have a medical degree, for your child you are the leading authority on health and illness, just about as good as any doctor.

Just like any good nurse or emergency-room doctor, your first task is to identify the symptoms. What does it feel like? Where is the pain coming from? How long has this been going on?

But watch out! After you've felt your child's forehead for a temperature, checked his neck for swollen glands, and had him stick out his tongue and say "Ahh!" you're liable to face a suddenly uncooperative patient.

Although you're only doing what any other healthcare professional would do in the same situation, as Dr. Mom, you are now expected to administer quick and efficient care—without bothering your child too much.

And if you approach the child with a thermometer, a wet rag, or any other form of annoyance, you can expect to hear those four familiar words.

Much like the doctor trying to learn the patient's symptoms, the only way to find out how your patient is feeling is to ask questions.

"Do you think you're going to throw up?"

"Want to try to eat a little something?"

"Let me give you a little of this cough syrup so you can sleep."

All met with—you guessed it.

As with any good doctor, once you have figured out the cause of the child's illness, the next step is to provide treatment. If you ask most mothers, a little TLC is the best medicine. But of course there will be many occasions when a child's illness calls for hot tea, a cold compress, or some nasty-tasting cough syrup.

Whether the prescribed treatment takes the form of hot tea, cold water and juices, hearty chicken noodle soup, a warm wash cloth on the child's forehead, a bag of ice pressed where the child skinned a knee, or a couple of aspirin, you will always run the risk of hearing that famous line.

How many times have you said an exchange like this one?

"Don't forget to keep the ice pressed against where it hurts."

"Did you take a couple Tylenol?"

"Did you finish your tea? Do you want some more?"

All met with silence until, when the child's patience has been tested to its absolute limits, you are met with the irritated response, "Mom, you're so *annoying*!"

And let's not forget the final, crucial part of your role as doctor and parent: following up with your patient. Just as a doctor tells her patient, "Take two of these and call me in the morning," as a loving and devoted mother you are naturally eager to see your child getting better. Has the swelling stopped? Is the nausea gone? Is the headache getting better or worse?

Now that the illness has gotten slightly better, there's an excellent chance that the child will be sick of hearing what to do to treat the illness, and sick of answering questions about it. The result? Being told, yet again, how annoying you are being!

It's all part of the parent's role, part of the endlessly repeating pattern of trying to care for and respect your child, make sure the child is comfortable and secure . . . only to be told, in no uncertain terms, that you're being a pain!

Oh, well. Look on the bright side: at least you don't have to send them a bill for your services. Just imagine how annoying you'd be then!

Chapter Eight

Personal Hygiene

A major struggle for many parents is the constant battle over personal hygiene. As a sensible adult you know how important it is not only for your child to be clean and presentable but for the child to learn good habits when it comes to personal hygiene. But the fact is, very few children are born with a strong, natural sense of the importance of cleaning themselves. Far more common is the child who'd love nothing better than to play in the dirt and go directly to bed, then get up the next morning and put on the same clothes he wore the day before. Personal hygiene, as much as the alphabet and good manners, is something that a parent must teach her child.

When your child is very young, difficulty over cleanliness might mean fights over taking a bath, brushing teeth, and struggles convincing the child to allow you to shampoo their hair or wash under their arms. Once your son or daughter reaches a certain age, the problem becomes even trickier: there's no way they'll let you see them naked, much less soap up their body with warm water and lift their arms and wash under them. A parent faces the double challenge of persuading the child to bathe regularly without being able to monitor how well the child actually does it—aside from conducting "the smell test," that is, and noticing any strong odors that might still remain after the child has showered!

But of course, cleanliness is not all about bathing. After the child has been playing outside, whether it's Barbies and jump rope out back or basketball at the park, it's crucial that he or she not come to the dinner table with dirty hands. The important thing for a parent is to build good habits that will carry the child through life—after all, it's not just about being presentable at the dinner table, but about killing off germs and viruses that wind up on your hands. Parents of toddlers know how quickly young children can get their hands into all kinds of dirty, sticky messes!

Of course, building any kind of habit in your child is not as simple as asking them to do something once or twice. No, whether it's washing their hands with warm water and soap, wiping dirt and sweat off their faces, or changing out of filthy, sweaty clothes after running around outside, "building good hygiene habits" might as well be the same as asking them to walk the dog or clean their room. But just as with any other important parental duty, a dedicated mother or father has no choice but to nag, warn, sweet-talk, and even threaten their child over and over again—no matter how many times it takes. You might even end up *agreeing* with your child when he or she responds, "You're so annoying!" You'll certainly think the child is right whenever you hear something like, "You told me that already!" But until the child actually gets the message, you'll at least have a witty response ready: "So why do I keep having to tell you?"

All of these struggles relating to showering, hand-washing, and general hygiene will eventually come to seem like a walk in the park, though, when the child enters the dreaded teenage years. While your young son or daughter may pick up any number of unpleasant odors from their adventures out in the world, it's only after puberty that they start actively *producing* strange smells of their very own. And yet for some strange reason, it seems that during this time of their life they're absolutely convinced that they don't have to wash regularly—or at least, that they desperately don't want to. Add to that the sudden, unexplained desire to wear the same pair of jeans every day, the same lucky t-shirt, and never to toss that sweater or hoodie in the laundry, and you've got a recipe not just for a foul-smelling child but one that's liable to be a breeding ground for all kinds of nasty germs.

It might sound like the same kind of challenge you faced when the child got old enough to bathe themselves—how do you get them to exercise good personal hygiene when you can't stand over them to make sure they actually do it? But no, it's harder than that, much harder—now you're dealing with a young person absolutely determined to do things their own way, and who might even be convinced you're going out of your way to embarrass and yell at them.

It's almost enough to make a parent want to use reverse psychology, and say, "You smell fine to me. No need to wash those clothes." Notice I said *almost*: this technique can backfire badly, when your teen smiles and says, "You see, I told you I didn't smell!"

Another aspect of personal hygiene that many parents find themselves fighting their children over is brushing their teeth. Even for an adult who knows firsthand the importance of good dental health, brushing two or three times a day, as well as using dental floss to get between the teeth, can be tedious. Imagine how a child must feel! And yet as a parent you have a responsibility to help your children develop good habits that will prevent them from going down a long road of dental problems and continuing dentist bills.

Unfortunately, the only way forward is to keep to the path, no matter how difficult that may sometimes become. Stressing the importance of good personal hygiene, from bathing to hand-washing to brushing and flossing their teeth, are the parent's job, and unfortunately you are stuck in the role until your child gets the message or leaves home—whichever comes first. Until then, all that parents can do is be persistent and be strong, and mentally prepare themselves for hearing all sorts of backlash from their children, from "Just leave me alone!" to "This doesn't need to be cleaned" and "I smell fine!"

Just as with bathing, brushing your child's teeth for them might be something you can get away with for a few years. At some point, however, you must leave the task up to your child. Unless you're okay with replacing half your child's teeth with metal fillings, you must be proactive, reminding the child to get the upper and lower teeth, and quite possibly standing by the sink watching to make sure those teeth actually get brushed. In my house, we would even use a red tablet that our kids would chew on, showing places where they didn't brush well.

The same way you'll hear all sorts of backtalk when you remind your child to bathe and wash their hands, you can guarantee you'll hear some pretty familiar comments when you insist that they go over those back teeth once more, and don't forget to brush the tongue. The good thing is that with their mouths full of toothpaste, you won't really hear the nasty things they are saying!! *Thank G-d!*

Chapter Nine

Chef

Of all the challenges parents face, one of the most surprising is the stress and additional work that children tend to cause where food is involved. When Mom has raised a child to the age of two or three, first on milk and then on pureed fruits and strained carrots, it can catch a mother off-guard to hear from her child that carrots are disgusting and chicken nuggets are the only acceptable dinner food from now on. Or from my own personal experience, macaroni and cheese was a favorite in my house—a store-bought plastic container which my son used to call "hom hom" and would eat so much of that he became sick, at which point I had to stop giving it to him. And of course, it doesn't help when the child expresses this opinion by tossing a platter of carrots onto the floor!

The moment when a child begins to express his or her own taste preferences it becomes fascinating, because often what your child likes to eat will be radically different from your own tastes. And it goes without saying that what the child likes will have no relation to what you like to cook, much less what is easiest and most convenient for you to cook! If your child suddenly develops a taste for lobster bisque or spinach quiche, you can bet the child is not going to spare much time thinking of how difficult these meals are to prepare!

When you scratch the surface of the task of feeding children, a number of different challenges come up. None is more important than looking after your children's nutrition and making sure that they get the vitamins and minerals they need. This can be trickier than it seems at first—once kids reach a certain age, they tend to refuse to eat certain foods, sometimes going so far as to hide them or even drop them beneath the table. Of course, they never seem to refuse foods like cookies, ice cream, and candy—rather, it's the sides of Brussel's sprouts, mushrooms, spinach, eggplant, peas, etc., etc., that they turn their noses up at. In other words, all the healthy stuff!

Chef Mom faces a tough challenge: how to cook nutritious foods so her kids grow up healthy and strong . . . but do it while making dishes tasty enough that her kids will actually want to eat these foods! It's an age-old problem, and there are answers out there—from withholding dessert or TV until the child's plate is clean to more devious methods like sneaking servings of vegetables into brownies! It's all about being creative and tricky as Chef/Mom. Eating healthy is a goal for us moms.

A closely related problem is the struggle to get the child to try new foods. We've all experienced a child who suddenly discovers pizza, or macaroni and cheese, or Sourpatch Kids, and decides that from here on in, no other foods will do. Heaven help the parent who insists that just for tonight, let's just try this healthy salad, full of fresh peppers and tomatoes. The mother who tries to give her child the gift of good nutrition might get an eardrum-piercing scream for her trouble, or might just hear those famous words: "Mom, you're so annoying!"

Of course, we also live in an age of almost-unlimited options when it comes to food. Food can be a wonderful gateway for children to explore other cultures, as well as offering a diversity of meals and flavors that earlier generations of parents could only dream of. While nutrition is key, there are many other reasons for a parent to want to get the child to explore new and interesting foods.

Sadly, none of these good reasons mean much to a child who just wants to eat pizza—*again*—for dinner. Try something new? Be exposed to an unfamiliar culture? No, thanks—just give him the pizza! And look out if you dig in your heels: you're liable to hear something along the lines of "I don't care what's in it" or "I don't care where it's from" or maybe "I don't want to eat that smelly crap!"

For Chef Mom, it's all part of the job description. And tempting as it may be to just give in, every sensible mom knows that it's far better to put up with the stress and torment of hearing your child's complaints than to raise a sickly, vitamin-deficient child—or for that matter, to have to tend to a pale, weak child who's constantly catching every cold and flu bug going around the school!

Of course, it's perfectly normal for children to get fixated on certain foods and to turn up their noses at other strange foods that they haven't tried before. Most times, kids will grow out of these phases as their taste buds grow and mature, allowing their preferences to expand. Nine times out of ten, a child's culinary tastes will expand naturally, and it will become a little easier to sneak some fruits and vegetables into their diet.

But there is always the possibility of that one-out-of-ten child known as The Picky Eater. Terrorizing parents for centuries, The Picky Eater is stubbornly committed to his tastes, and will try new, unfamiliar dishes only after Chef Mom has worn him down with pleas, promises, and threats—and then, almost inevitably, he will make a face and set down his fork, refusing to eat more than the one or two bites he's taken so far. While other children are trying new things and admitting that apples taste good, and yes, a bowl of Asian stir-fry can be quite tasty, The Picky Eater remains absolutely committed to those few things that he's absolutely sure he likes.

In some cases, sadly, picky eating is a lifelong condition, and the child may grow into an adult who still dislikes fruit and vegetables. Still, it is Chef Mom's duty to try, and when necessary to take extreme measures such as bargaining with the child, making deals—dessert for three bites of broccoli—and even outright threatening the child. Tough love doesn't stop just because it's dinnertime. With persistence, Chef Mom can sometimes get through to the child and convince him or her to eat an occasional salad, or suffer through eating a banana or a few strawberries.

That's not to say it will be pretty, of course. Chef Mom is certain to be left holding a forkful of healthy food, turned away from a tightly closed mouth. And it's guaranteed that she'll hear a few nasty comments along the way, from "Let me eat what I want!" and "Your cooking is so gross!" to that old, familiar classic, "Mom, you're so annoying!"

Chapter Ten

Fashion Designer

Just like a safe, happy home, keeping the child clothed is one of a parent's most important responsibilities. It sounds so simple, doesn't it? But just as a child will suddenly decide that carrots and bananas are disgusting, children have a funny way of suddenly changing their fashion sense, sometimes in the blink of an eye. It can be enough to drive a parent crazy, but of course there's nothing a mother or father can do but try to accommodate the child as best they can—hopefully without going broke or crazy in the process.

The parent's responsibility to clothe the child begins at the hospital, when the newborn is dressed in "receiving clothes" for the ride home, which is a whole production in itself! For the next few years, fortunately, keeping the child dressed is not too difficult, and even fun. There isn't anything more adorable than baby clothes, from "onesies" to matching outfits, tiny dresses, and miniature baby shoes that fit in the palm of your hand. The most important thing of all, though, is that the child doesn't speak, and so you don't have to worry about complaints about what they like or don't like. Everything goes smooth for Mom.

As the child gets older, the struggles with clothes change dramatically. Some parents may find that for their children, wearing clothes at all is too much to ask—look away for two seconds, and you're liable to see your child running around naked! Everything comes off, or everything is put on all at once.

Jarring color combinations, stripes and polka dots worn together, winter clothes during the summer—the fashion sense of a small child is a little different from yours or my sense of style. They don't care what is wrong or right, what matches or doesn't. Some children suddenly get the idea that they must wear their special pajama pants, even if the family is going to a fancy dinner. If you don't believe it, just try explaining to a four-year-old that she can't wear her Halloween costume to school today! Good luck!

Parents have one other big challenge to worry about as their children grow older: keeping them in clothes that fit! From the time they're born, almost up until they graduate high school, children grow at a rapid rate that means they need new clothes every few years, if not more frequently. If a parent is very lucky, there are hand-me-downs to hand down from one child to the next. More often than not, however, taking the child to the store, looking for clothes in the next size up, is a never-ending job—and a very expensive one!

By the time the child hits puberty, they'll most likely have a strong group of friends and care deeply about what their peers think. That means that all of a sudden, the pants and shirt you pull off the rack for them to try on are going to be completely ridiculous—totally ugly and out of style. Of course, your child might not come right out and tell you this—they're just as likely to roll their eyes at that sweater you just pulled off the rack, or they may say, "Mom, you don't know what the kids wear today!"

It's your job as a parent to decipher their meaning, just as it's your job to figure out what clothes they *will* wear. What are their friends wearing? If you're lucky, it's something simple, easy to find, and not incredibly expensive. If you're unlucky, though, you could be hunting through store after store for the latest fashion fad, designer goods with a price tag to match, or the impossible to find because every store is sold out of the item.

And if you thought kids physically outgrew clothes quickly, you haven't seen anything until you've looked into a teenager's closet, how they outgrew clothes that were cool last year and are long forgotten. Something the child begged to have just a few months ago might be totally out of style by the end of the season. As a parent, it's your job to balance your child's desire to dress in a way that makes them feel comfortable and confident against the need to not go crazy or broke along the way.

All parents have to find that balance for themselves. Along with price, a parent may have to put their foot down over other concerns as well. If the current trend is very short skirts or skimpy shorts for girls, a parent has to decide whether to allow her daughter to leave the house in such clothes. For boys, t-shirts with rude or suggestive messages sometimes become hot trends—are you, as that boy's parents, going to let him go to school wearing a t-shirt like that? Putting your foot down may mean starting a big fight over the child's clothes, and even over other things—don't be surprised if the child reacts angrily, saying things like, "You never let me do what I want!" or "Everyone is wearing that. Why can't you just let me wear what I want to wear?" And of course, you can expect to hear that all-time classic, "Everybody is wearing that!"

One of the toughest challenges is clothing your children, especially when they become teenagers.

That means not saying anything when your teen wants a silly haircut, wants to wear big floppy pants or some kind of crazy outfit, and not pointing out that in six months or a year they'll be embarrassed they ever went out in such attire.

Slip up and point any of this out to your child when they want to wear it, and you can be sure of hearing that familiar line: "Mom, you're so annoying! You don't know what kids are wearing today!"

Chapter Eleven

Lifeguard

Going to the beach or pool is one of the greatest pleasures of summer. Anyone who grew up near an ocean or a lake will be full of strong memories of swimming as a child, being outdoors with friends and family by the water. One of the great gifts a parent can give to their own children is taking them to the beach to create memories of their own.

The flipside of that, though, is the anxiety a parent feels when introducing their child to the water. Whether it's the beach, Atlantic Ocean, a calm lake in the middle of the woods, or even just the swimming pool at the local YMCA, water presents a serious danger for children, especially when they're just learning to swim or can't swim at all.

Swimming lessons, camps for young swimmers, and thousands of swimming aids like rafts, paddle boards, and "water wings" all exist because of this widespread fear. But still they're not enough to calm a nervous parent—that's why you'll often find parents on the beach, far from relaxing with a book or taking a nap, you'll find them anxiously sitting up, keeping their eyes on their children at all times. It's not a very calming way to vacation!

Parents feel a responsibility to keep their children safe from all dangers. When it comes to the beach, they mostly do that by staying close, wading into the waves with their children and carrying them out when they've gotten in too deep.

Of course, the beach has many other dangers, from sunburn and sharp shells and stones to the mere fact that it's a giant public place, and your child may be frolicking in the surf alongside all kinds of strangers. For the anxious parent of a younger child, there's no shortage of things to get the heart racing! G-d forbid you hear anything in the news about polluted water or, scariest of all, shark sightings in the area!

At some point, of course, children become too big to pick up and carry out of danger, and independent enough to want to go play in the water by themselves, or with friends.

At that point, a parent has no choice but to let the child go. As a parent at that moment, you just hope that the child will remember everything you've taught them about staying safe, from avoiding rip tides and treading water when they're out among the waves, to avoiding talking with strangers and remembering where the family's blankets are set up.

Of course, it's not always easy to just let the child go. Many parents will still play the role of lifeguard no matter how old their children get, glancing out over their book or lowering their sunglasses to scan the surf, just making sure their child is still there, still doing okay.

And of course as parents it's our nature to want to offer one last word of advice before the child goes trotting off into the water: "Remember to look out for jellyfish" or "Don't go out too far this time," along with a hundred other warnings.

Even when the child comes back from the waves, the advice doesn't end: "Put on some sunscreen" and "Drink some water so you don't get dehydrated."

As always, the parent means well. But that won't stop the child from replying, "I know what I'm doing," "I'm not a baby," "I can take care of myself," "Stop it already," or those four famous words.

Am I really that annoying???

Chapter Twelve

Sex and Dating

Watching your children grow up is one of the most fulfilling things about being a parent—and one of the hardest, most rewarding jobs there is. It's impossible not to look at this child becoming his or her own person, developing thoughts and opinions of their own, and figuring out the world around them. For some parents it's even difficult to accept that time is passing, and the child who clung to you not so long ago is now a teenager who doesn't want to be seen in public with you because it's embarrassing when they see their friends when they're with their parents.

Nothing demonstrates this bittersweet challenge more than the parent's responsibility of telling their child about sex and dating, better known as "the birds and the bees," and getting them ready for the frightening world of dating, love, and sex. Of all the things a parent will teach their child, these are some of the most important lessons. Teaching the right thing, and instilling good values and morals when it comes to dating and romance.

But at the same time, seeing that your child is interested in dating can be a difficult pill for a parent to swallow. Your little baby is growing up, and soon they will be an adult. In fact, it's possible that before long your child will be leaving the house, will be married, will have a baby of their own. It can seem like childhood is over all of a sudden—a sad, depressing thought.

Just as with the parent's many other difficult but required tasks, though, it's your job to make sure the child learns right from wrong—no matter how annoying, gross, or nosy the child may tell you you are being!

41

The first challenge for a parent is to give the child a basic sense of how things work—in other words, "the birds and the bees." Parents have a big decision to make simply deciding *when* to give their children "the talk." Make sure they hear this information from you before one of their friends gives them a "lesson" on this topic in the playground at school.

If you give them the "birds and bees" lecture too early, it might go in one ear and out the other. On the other hand, if you wait too long you face the opposite danger: a confused child coming to you with questions about something they overheard in the locker room or on the bus. It's not usually difficult to set the child straight, but you may as well tell them the truth about where babies come from before they get attached to the wild and crazy tales they're likely to pick up from their friends. A parent who waits too long runs the risk of a child who's in the midst of puberty without even knowing what is happening to their body.

It's easy to understand why a parent would hesitate before giving their child a talk on the birds and the bees. The information might be startling and even upsetting to a child, especially if they've accepted that babies come from storks, or any other explanation you've given them up until now. Depending on their age, you must give appropriate information.

It's often a very uncomfortable conversation for the parent as well! Some of the details, especially the description of sexual intercourse, may be awkward to share with your child—especially if you are prone to remembering your children as tiny, innocent babies.

And if you describe puberty and the body's changes, it can feel a little like you are giving your child terrible news. Just imagine if someone took you aside and told you that very soon you were going to start growing hair in unexpected places, your voice was going to start changing, and you were going to start having feelings for people you'd always thought were disgusting! It's not a pleasant thing to hear.

But once you've given your child "the talk," you can breathe a little easier. You've laid a good foundation for everything that comes next.

In a way, the part of sex and puberty is the easiest for your child to understand. What can be scary, and even gross, is the idea that they are suddenly going to want to kiss a member of the opposite sex, who they've probably gone their entire lives thinking were completely disgusting.

Try explaining to your child about what you think about how and when to ask the opposite sex if they would like to go to a movie, skating, out for ice cream, etc., etc. You'll be sure to hear, "Mom, I know! Stop, you don't have to tell me!"

This can be a difficult task for any parent—not only is it tricky to give good advice, but you have to be careful about giving too much advice, or showing *too much* interest in your child's romantic life. Sure, your child may have come to you to ask what to do about having a terrible crush on someone in pre-algebra class, but if you ask too many questions or, G-d forbid, bring the matter up later on, you can count on hearing some version of "Mom, you're embarrassing me!" or "None of your business" or, of course, four famous words.

Giving your child dating advice can be a golden opportunity to create good habits in your child. Your son may think that the girl he's taking out will be thrilled to go see the latest action-adventure movie, or spend two hours in an arcade, but this is your chance to gently point out that that might not be what a teenage girl is interested in.

"What do you think she would like to do?" can be a kinder, gentler way of telling your child to think about other people and their interests—which doesn't exactly come naturally to the average teenager!

When it comes to actually asking the other person on a date, it can be difficult for a parent to really put themselves in the child's shoes. It may have been several decades since you last had to ask someone out. The butterflies in the stomach, the sweaty palms, the rapid heartbeat may be just distant memories to you, but they're all too real to your child. A parent who forgets this and tells the child to "Just do it," or asks, "What's the worst that can happen?" is liable to hear some snappy comments or remarks from their child: "Oh, you think this is easy? This is serious," and "It's not that simple," or "What happens if they say no?" It must be so scary. It breaks your heart thinking that your child can get hurt.

When you have to go through this with your child, you have to watch what you say, what you ask, what you don't ask, and how you say it or ask it. If it's not done in a way that's to your child's liking, you'll be sure to hear how you don't understand kids today.

If the beginning of a new romance for your child can be challenging, just wait until your child goes through their first break-up. Even for a parent who's been married for decades, watching a son or daughter go through the agony of having a relationship end—especially if your child is on the receiving end of the break-up—will make you feel as if your heart has just been ripped out.

Needless to say, it's up to you, as a parent, to be there to listen as your child suffers through the agony of losing love and the humiliation of being "dumped." You're the one to simply listen as your child goes over everything again and again and again and again. You have to show compassion, understanding, and interest.

Of course, your child might react very differently and hole up in their bedroom, refusing to leave, even to eat dinner, shower, or come downstairs to watch their favorite TV show. In that case, it will be your job to prepare meals you can leave beside the bedroom door, returning later to collect the dirty dishes. You'll have to make a difficult decision about whether to indulge your child completely, or put your foot down when they haven't showered in four days, and you can start to smell them from outside their room! They have to go through the mourning process.

However your child responds to the end of a relationship, this is an important parenting moment. Until that first relationship comes to its inevitable end, your child may believe that dating and romance are all sunshine and rainbows—in other words, easy. Helping comfort your child through a break-up is a golden opportunity to break the news that relationships can be difficult, and require both sides to put in some effort if they're going to work. And of course it's a good time to let your child know that there are "plenty of fish in the sea" and that they may have to kiss a few frogs before they find their prince (or princess). Even that is something you have to explain. So here we go again, another hat we must wear: therapist?

But as with other times when you may give your child advice, be careful! While the aftermath of a break-up seems like the best time to share some hard truths about romance and to let your child know that everyone goes through these heartaches, your child may not see it that way. If you are the parent of a teenager, you know how prone they can be to drama. Telling your heartbroken child that this break-up is all for the best and it will be better in the long run could result in your child screaming at a high volume, "You don't have any idea what I'm going through!" or "I'll never love anyone again!"

Never mind that you've had far more life experience, and perhaps even dated other people before you met the child's other parent—if your child is in a certain mood, there's simply nothing you can say. Keep trying to help them, and you might be setting yourself up to hear that timeless line . . . and you know what it is!

If you somehow thought that was all there was to the topic of guiding your child through the world of romance, you are in for a shock. The biggest and trickiest topic is still ahead: sex, and talking to your child about sex.

It can be enough to make a parent break into a cold sweat. The thought of sitting your teenager down and discussing what a serious commitment sex is, much less explaining how condoms work or even demonstrating how to put one on, can cause nightmares for many parents and children. For parents who may still be recovering from giving the "birds and bees" talk, even years later, the thought of talking frankly to your child about sex can seem like something that has to be talked about, but how do you approach it?

One big reason is simply the discomfort the average parent is bound to have at the very thought of their precious child, their little baby, being sexually active. It can be a sad and even shocking thought—not to mention how old it may make you feel!

The other big reason is knowing how uncomfortable it will make your child, and the fact that you are bound to hear comments like "Mom, that's disgusting!" or "I don't want to talk about this! I learned all that in school!"

But of course, a parent's job is never done, and having this talk with your child may be the difference between being a very caring and concerned mom to a very annoying mom. To the point of even hearing your child say, "Do you try to think of things to purposely annoy me?!" While you're thinking that you're just trying to be a great parent. They'll get it one day!

Chapter Thirteen

Drinking

As your child gets older, you'll face the bittersweet situation of watching them grow into a confident and adventurous young person with a mind of their own and an active social life.

Why is this bittersweet? After all, if your child is making friends and enjoying new experiences, that means they're growing into a happy and well-adjusted young person—meaning you've done a good job as a parent!

On the other hand, you'll probably begin to miss the child years. You may begin to think back fondly to the days when the child was young and couldn't bear to be out of your sight, and now they are sometimes embarrassed to be seen with you. While you probably will and will not miss the temper tantrums and your child jumping into your bed at three in the morning, many parents get sad at the idea that their child no longer wants to do the same things with you as they did when they were little.

A bigger problem, though, is the fear of the different dangers your child may get into when they venture out into the world. Some of these worries might just be a fear of the unknown—it's a scary world, of course, so advice like looking both ways when you cross the street and never talking to strangers will always make sense (even if it prompts the child to tell you how annoying you're being!).

Along with some of these fears, with sex being one of the big ones, is the thought of drinking! What parent in their right mind *wouldn't* worry that their teenager, whose judgment might not be the best to begin with, is out somewhere drinking something that lowers their inhibitions and makes their decision-making process even worse? Then getting into a car after a few drinks? YIKES!

The whole matter brings up a big dilemma for parents. In a perfect world, you could tell your teenager, "Don't drink until you're twenty-one!" It's good advice, and it would certainly keep them out of trouble. But if you're like most parents, can you really depend on your child to do what you tell them?!

If the answer is "No," you're faced with a tough decision: whether or not to come down hard on your child, implementing a curfew and even going so far as to smell their breath and clothes when they come home late at night. If you do any of those things, be prepared to hear lots of remarks about how unfair and mistrustful you're being!

If you're not prepared to do those things, then you've just got to trust your child, hoping that everything that you taught them sunk in. That doesn't mean you have to send them off to the next beer party or unsupervised house party willingly.

If you decide that your child is probably going to drink, your best bet is to make sure they're prepared to face the realities of alcohol and its many side issues so that they can be well prepared for the various situations they may face. So, you sit down with them and talk about all the details.

As with so many other parenting situations, this is going to involve you sitting your child down to hear what you've got to say, all the information you have to give them, especially if they really don't want to hear it. By now, of course, you're probably an old pro at hearing complaints like "I know what I'm doing," "I'm not even going to drink," and "Why don't you trust or believe me?" and of course, "Mom, you're so annoying!" and not letting it bother you.

There are many issues to go over when it comes to teens and drinking. Especially when your child or their friends may be new drivers, the threat of drunk driving is always very real. While you don't want to make your child too terrified, it's crucial that you instill in them a clear understanding of all the terrible things that could happen if they get behind the wheel after drinking, or ride in a car with someone who has. Talking to them about putting their drink down unattended, the dangers that could happen, for them to tell you "Nobody is going to do that" and you having to explain how it happens. Sometimes, it's done as a joke or a goof, but it's really not. That could turn into a really serious situation, and that's something you have to explain. There are lots of statistics available of kids just like them who thought they were invincible, who had just one drink, who made one stupid mistake, and now are no longer with us. It can be sad for the parent, as well as the child, to face these tragic cases, but it's worth discussing if it will help your child make the right decision later on.

Another important issue for you to talk about is simply the need for your child to know their own limits when it comes to drinking. Cases of alcohol poisoning, and even teens dying from drinking too much, are unfortunately all too common. And even if you trust your child not to go that far, it's important that they respect—and even fear—the power of alcohol. Unfortunately, many teenagers learn only from experience what a hangover feels like, or how unpleasant it is to vomit into the bushes after drinking too much.

Some of these conversations might be as uncomfortable for you as they are for your child. Surely no parent has ever enjoyed having to spend time thinking about their child being injured in a drunk-driving accident, having their stomach pumped at a hospital after binge drinking, or being drugged by a stranger.

But as much as your child may hate it, and as annoying you may seem to them, it's a parent's duty to share these uncomfortable truths with their child.

Chapter Fourteen

Detective

You might have thought that your duties as an officer of the law were over when it came time to being a judge.

Not so fast. As every mom knows, a key job requirement for parents is being a detective. Figuring things out, where, why, who, and how. We don't stop until we get an answer.

Who drew on the walls with a purple crayon? Who stuck their finger in the cake? Who put a bright red t-shirt in the washing machine with the white sheets and towels? Who drank the last of the milk and put an empty container back in the refrigerator?

The list of cases never ends for Mom the Detective. When your children are young to when they become teenagers, from small cases to big cases. You may find yourself investigating escapes: how did your one-year-old get out of their crib? When they're older, you'll be dealing with vandalism and petty theft: who left a chocolate handprint on the back of Mom's dress? Who stole the cookie from the cookie jar?

For the first few years of your children's lives, the cases won't be too tough to crack. You'll usually have a pretty good idea of who left the candy fingerprints on those important papers you left lying around—and if you don't, you can probably follow a trail of candy-colored "tracks" back to the suspect.

But as your children get older, they become a little more sophisticated about covering their tracks.

Cases get harder, and you have to deal with a big obstacle: now that your kids can talk, they're able to offer up alibis and excuses for why it couldn't have been them who left that enormous mess in the kitchen.

If you have a few children, you'll also have to figure out situations where you have to use your best detective skills to find out what *really* happened in a dispute or fight between them. One child claims they weren't doing anything at all when the other one came up and punched them. The other one says that their sibling was teasing them. Who do you believe, and how do you get to the bottom of the matter?

Every mom has to build up her own detective skills, developing tricks and techniques that will help her crack cases for years to come. Some of the most common tools include:

*Physical evidence: Even when your children are past the age of leaving handprints on the walls and trails of dirt and mud behind them, there are lots of physical "clues" you can pick up on . . . and chances are you won't even need a magnifying glass to find them! Things like dirty shoes and clothes, the contents of their pockets, and even papers they might leave lying around all can provide the evidence you'll need to get to the bottom of what's really going on.

Nowadays, most kids use e-mail, social media, and cell phones. If you really need to get to the heart of a case, these are all key areas to look for clues like text messages, suspicious phone calls, and even e-mails where you're liable to find a "confession" in black and white.

For many moms, interrogation might be the first and best technique for getting to the heart of a case. Unlike detectives on television, using harsh methods like yelling, most moms have a "Mom Look" they can turn on their children that lets them know play time is over, and if they don't tell the truth there are really going to be problems.

If "the Look" by itself isn't enough to get the job done, Mom the Detective's next best bet is to make promises and threats. Fortunately for Mom the Detective, you have a lot of leverage when it comes to taking away privileges and possessions: promise to cut a child off from TV, cell phone, social media, and even real-life time with friends, and you might then have a very talkative suspect on your hands!

If all else fails, Mom the Detective can always bring in her partner, Dad the Detective, and play that classic game "Good Cop, Bad Cop." In many families, Dad will slide naturally into the role of Bad Cop, but as mentioned above,

Mom can be a pretty convincing Bad Cop when she flashes "that Mom Look" at the child.

Moms have a way and have sources of finding things out that Dad doesn't ever know and never will. Moms go to that next step—the Mom Step: the step that Dad would never go to! Moms should have their own TV show: *Criminal Moms* instead of *Criminal Minds*!

Of course, not all of Mom the Detective's work will be centered on a crime the child has committed or a dispute between children. Some of Mom the Detective's most important work, in fact, comes before a crime has even been committed. With her fine-tuned sense of when her children are up to something, as well as her toolkit of detective's tools, some of Mom's best detecting comes when the child is thinking of doing something they shouldn't. When they're up to no good.

When it comes to paying attention to trouble your child might be up to, Mom the Detective has a few tools at her disposal besides having eyes behind her head. When I tell my kids that, they look at me like I'm nuts, and I hear them mumble to each other, "What does that mean?"

First is snooping: paying attention to clues like odd behavior, strange body language, or a sudden desire for secrecy. These are like red flashing warning signs to Mom the Detective, activating her sense of trouble on the horizon.

Second is simply asking questions. Many children will find themselves unable to spin a web of lies when Mom the Detective asks them difficult questions. Nine times out of ten, the child's scheme will come to light, or else the child will realize Mom the Detective has caught wind of their plans, and they'll think twice about carrying out whatever bit of trouble they were planning.

Third, if questions don't do the job, is to set a trap for the child. Often, Mom the Detective will be able to figure out exactly what the child has planned. In order to prevent them from doing others or themselves any real harm, Mom might do something like pretend to leave the house and drive halfway down the street, then double back and sneak into the house to catch the child red-handed. It's a sneaky tactic, but it works! Or go to our secret sources and get the information we need.

Just as with searching your child's room, going through their journal, or listening in on their phone calls, this tactic can be risky. You might find yourself hearing those old stand-bys "Mom, you're so annoying!" and "You never give me any privacy!" or even "You never trust me."

"You always think I'm up to something!" and "Why can't you just trust me?" are among the many cries you can expect to hear if you prevent trouble from occurring.

And of course if you've really hit a nerve with your prediction, you can expect to hear an unusually loud sigh. "Oh, you just don't stop!"

Compared to these duties, one of the easier tasks Mom the Detective is responsible for is finding lost items around the house. While this may sound simpler than resolving a dispute, though, finding objects can be tricky—especially when you have to dig through the mess in your child's room to find the object!

Sometimes, finding things can be a simple task. "Where did you last see it?" is a classic question that often helps give your investigation some direction. And Mom the Detective will be able to consult with Mom the Laundry Queen and Mom the Chauffeur to see if the missing object has gone through the wash or is out in the car. Mom the Cleaning Lady might also be able to remember if she's seen the missing item in the last few days. We get blamed anyway because we are accused of putting it somewhere when cleaning up

One of Mom the Detective's best tools for finding lost items is simply knowing her children well. Maybe the child is always losing socks behind the radiator, or books tend to disappear under their bed. In many cases, Mom's knowledge of her kids will lead her on the right path to the lost item.

Just be prepared to face some opposition along the way. You are likely to hear some howls of annoyance when you ask your child whether they're *sure* it isn't in their book bag, or suggest that they look *just one more time* under the bed.

You can be sure to hear "Mom, you said that already," "I told you, I already looked there! Why don't you ever listen?" and of course, "Do you say these things to purposely annoy me?"

Chapter Fifteen

Gadgets

If you're like most parents, you've probably lost track of all the gadgets floating around your house. From television remotes to cell phones, tablets, high-tech watches, and video-game systems, it's probably been years since you could identify every electronic device your kids use.

When you aren't annoying your kids asking them to put away this or that electronic, you're probably making them laugh by trying to turn the television on with the remote control for the DVD player, or trying in vain to talk into a handheld video-game player that looks just like your cell phone.

Gadgets are one of the areas where there's the greatest distance between parents and kids, and the gap is getting wider all the time. When you were a child, you probably had a television, a record player, a radio . . . and not much more. If you were very lucky, you might have had a word processor or even a computer in the home.

Compare that to the tremendous range of electronics any kid today will have access to. Computers, smart phones, tablets, e-readers, Netflix, iPods, digital cable with 500 channels and thousands of movies and television shows just waiting to be viewed. It's incredible what their minds can absorb, and what children have gotten used to in just a generation or so.

If you want to see the limits of your child's imagination when it comes to technology, though, try an experiment: tell them that when you were their age, not only did you not have the internet, you had to use an actual typewriter to type up papers for school. After you've said that, stand back and watch the blank expressions come over their faces—they simply won't understand what you're talking about! They'll even tell you how weird that is.

Your children have access to information and world experiences by the touch of a button. But the idea of watching only three television channels, or having to listen to the radio and hope their favorite song comes on, will make them feel like they're being tortured and how they could never have lived like that!

It can be an incredible reminder of how fast the world has changed. Never mind the fact that there was no Wikipedia, no chatting or e-mailing with friends, and no YouTube videos to get tips on how to write a good essay—there was no anything back then! You didn't even have a computer to print anything out on.

When you explain to your children how people talked to each other, how people looked one another in the eyes when we spoke, how it was so warm and personal. You explain how kids played in the street and how kids jumped rope and played ball and rode bikes and played outside. It was a friendly, happy atmosphere. We never needed gadgets to have a good time. When you explain how we read books, went to the library, when we figured things out for ourselves, instead of pressing a button on one of our many gadgets, it made life that much more fun, challenging, and rewarding. And the funny thing is that when I tell my kids this, they said they wish they knew what it was like to grow up in the time I did. They say that it sounds like it was so much warmer and more fun back then. It seemed like everybody was one big happy family.

With all that being said, technology is very welcomed and accepted today by people of all ages. So you still have to watch what you say about all these gadgets because your kids will still roll their eyes at you when you say anything negative about technology, and they'll still tell you how annoying you are being when you complain about all the new gadgets they keep coming out with every few months.

Chapter Sixteen

Etc., Etc., Etc.

As you can see by now, a parent wears many hats when it comes to raising children.

Some hats are easily identifiable, like a chef's hat or a policeman's cap. Others are harder to see, like the hat a parent slips on to tell their child about "the birds and the bees."

What many new parents don't fully appreciate is all the other miscellaneous hats a parent is called upon to wear. The hats are as different and as unexpected as kids themselves can be—meaning you never know which hat you're going to be called upon to wear at any given moment!

With that in mind, here are just a few of the other hats a parent might expect to wear over the course of raising their child. No list could ever be complete, and if you're reading this as a parent you'll no doubt think of a few hats you've had to wear as your child has grown from being a baby to a fully grown young adult.

Party Planner

Your child's birthday is coming up, and they have an idea in their head of what their party should look like. It doesn't matter if you don't have a big enough back yard for a pony. It doesn't matter if there are no stores in a 100-mile radius that sell the decorations, candy, soda, cakes, or games your child insists absolutely must be at the party. It doesn't matter if you don't even understand the party idea your child is trying to communicate.

None of this matters—as your child's party planner, it's up to you to make the party happen just as your child envisions it. And if you don't, well, you can expect to see some tears, and you may have a temper tantrum on your hands.

As party planner, your job isn't just to think big, designing the overall concept of the party. No, you've also got to think small—as in all the tiny details that throwing a successful party requires. That starts with the invitation list, going over it with your child and trying to figure out who they want at the party . . . and who you probably need to invite just to be polite.

Then it's time to pick out just the right invitations. If your child is picky, this might be a long process of suggesting this or that stationery, accepting it when your child tells you that these princess-themed invitations are stupid and the race car invitations are for little kids, before you come up with a winner.

Now all you've got to do is fill out the invitations, address them, and lick the envelopes. But that should be easy because your child will help you. Right? Noooo!

Once the invitations are out and you know how many kids will be coming over to tear your house apart—oops, coming over to celebrate your child's birthday—you can get started preparing for the party. That means making hundreds of trips to the supermarket for snacks and drinks, and another dozen trips to the party supply store for balloons, streamers, decorative paper plates, and so on.

If you've decided to hire any entertainment for the party, that's a whole other process. You'll probably spend a lot of time on the phone making sure the clown or balloon artist or celebrity impersonator can make it to the party on time, double-checking that your deposit check cleared, and then confirming that the entertainer hasn't backed out at the last minute—leaving you with a dozen or more restless children to contend with!

Once all of that is arranged, it's time to prepare your house for the party. You can't expect your child to help you blow up balloons, hang streamers, or tape up banners and signs wishing them a happy birthday . . . but you can definitely count on them chiming in with comments: "A little to the left with that banner," "More streamers over there," and "You have too many red balloons."

It's enough to make a parent want to yell, "Kids, you're so annoying!"

When the first guests arrive, your role changes completely. You've got to be a good host to your child's friends, offering them snacks, food, drinks, and making sure no one feels left out. That goes double for your child, the guest of honor. The worst thing that can happen at your child's birthday party is for them to feel like no one is paying attention to them. If that happens, you may be in for a meltdown, requiring you to call a dozen parents to come pick their kids up early. And if those parents are anything like you, they were probably really looking forward to a few hours of peace and quiet at home!

Being a good party planner and host means keeping the party moving along. You don't want to make your child wait too long to open presents, and you definitely don't want to give the other kids a chance to get bored and restless. If that happens, you'd just better hope that you put away all your valuables, because there's a good chance someone's going to run around the house, throw a ball indoors, or otherwise misbehave, knocking over your valuable vases and china.

When the party's all over, your job isn't quite done yet. That's right: now it's time to clean up!

Activity Planner

The good thing about your party planner hat is that the job is not too different from the role of activity planner. A parent who's been through a disastrous birthday party will probably learn some valuable lessons about what to do and not do when it comes to taking their child on a day trip to the zoo, or arranging a play date with a friend from school. And the challenges and struggles of planning a party will make it easier to arrange a play date for your child.

Nothing is ever really *easy* when it comes to raising children, is it?

Part of your job as an activity planner is to come up with ideas. This is where you get to really be creative with your child. But you've got to get used to hearing "No" and going back to the drawing board for more ideas.

Does your child want to go to the museum? No. Doesn't a walk down to the park sound fun? No. Wouldn't it be fun to go hear a concert? No. It's exhausting, and you didn't even go anywhere yet!

When you've finally suggested an activity your child would be willing to do, now comes the part where you work out all the details. When will you go, and when will you come back? If you are going to be out during a mealtime, should you prepare some food to bring along? If it's going to get cold later on, which jacket should you bring? If there's anything you can bet on as a parent, it's that your child is not going to be responsible for these details! So you'd better be.

Putting together a "play date" for your child can be a great way to relieve some pressure. Your child is going over a friend's house for the afternoon? Great! Let that kid's mom figure out how to keep the kids entertained for the next several hours.

Of course, the play date cuts both ways. You can't send your child to friends' houses every single time . . . as much as you might like to! Eventually, you are going to have to play the role of host to friends, and then the pressure is right back on you to figure out a fun activity for the afternoon—or, heaven help you, overnight in the case of a sleepover party!

Sleepovers

The sleepover is a challenge of its own. For many kids, a sleepover is fun because the parents let them have the basement and they can stay up all night watching movies, eating candy and drinking soda, and entertaining themselves. But until your kids reach that age, a sleepover is going to be a big production. It will take a lot more than just ordering pizza and buying a few bottles of soda and letting them have the run of your television. You'll have to watch over them, making sure everyone is comfortable and has enough room to sleep. And the odds are very good that in the middle of the night you might hear a knock on your door, with the news that one of your child's friends is now scared, and needs you to drive them back home. Time to put on your chauffeur's hat!

One of the nicer things about your child growing up is that at a certain point, figuring out what to do and who to do it with becomes something they don't want your help with. In fact, by the time your child becomes a teenager, they may not welcome your suggestion that they go ice skating or bowling—in those cases, be prepared for some eye rolling, and to hear snickering behind your back.

But that doesn't mean you're off the hook when it comes to playing a meaningful role in your child's social life. Naturally, you'll still be expected to drive the child to the mall, a friend's house, a school dance, or wherever, and then arrive promptly to pick them up. Oh, and don't forget that you're not to ask any questions about how the child's night went, who they talked to, what they did, etc., etc., etc.! If you do, you can bet on getting a reply from the back seat along the lines of "Mom, you're so nosey!" or "It's my business who I talked to! You don't know them!"

Social Coordinator

One of your most important jobs as an activity planner is keeping track of your child's calendar. That includes parties, sleepovers, and other social events.

But it also means knowing when your child has a test coming up, when a big project is due at school, etc. G-d forbid you ever forget one of these events—you won't get a lot of sympathy from your child. After all, it's *obviously* your job to keep track of when an important project is due, because it's going to be your fault anyway!

Add to play dates and tests the need to keep track of the different events your child has to go to, whether it's soccer practice or band rehearsal, and you can see that keeping your child's calendar can be a big undertaking. Now just imagine the complexity of being the schedule-keeper for a few children! It's enough to make you wish you had a personal assistant just to keep track of things.

Fundraiser

Chances are good that at some point in your child's life, they are going to want to have a lemonade stand or bake sales, another method of raising some money on their own. Bake sales are always fun: selling our baked goods at the park and having our friends join us for a fun-filled day of picnicking, playing, and enjoying a great afternoon. What made it even better was that the kids knew that the money raised went towards a good cause and they did a good deed.

Another great way of raising money for a good cause is the old classic lemonade stand. Showing and helping your children make the lemonade, setting up the tables and the pitchers and cups. Watching your kids sell lemonade to neighbors and people who stop by. Discussing with your children the proper amount to charge for a cup of lemonade. Running a lemonade stand can be a great way for your child to learn the basics of business and the importance of hard work.

But beware, because it also has the potential to backfire. Many parents have found themselves serving lemonade to customers with no children in sight, and later dismantling the lemonade stand while their child watches television or naps. And many more parents have ended up shelling out their own money for a pitcher of lemonade that never sold.

If your child is involved in clubs at school, chances are that running a lemonade stand won't be the last fundraising you're ever called upon to do.

You'd better keep some of your best baking recipes handy, because you are likely going to find yourself called upon to pitch in when the school takes part in that age-old tradition, the bake sale!

Get ready to slave over a dish of brownies or chocolate chip cookies in a hot kitchen while your child plays outside or hangs out with friends. And your contributions to the success of the club that your child belongs to is going to have to be your main reward for all your hard work—chances are that it will never occur to your child to say "Thank you," and that compliments and thanks passed on from other parents will never reach you.

That's if you're lucky enough to get away with just baking the items for the sale, and not going and sitting at the table, making change and handing over sweets. Good luck if you're asked to man the bake-sale table—say "No" and you'll look unfriendly, and you can be sure your child will respond with remarks like "Why do you have to be so selfish" and "Mom, you never do anything to help me!"

Storyteller

Finally, one of the greatest roles any parent is called upon to play is that of storyteller.

Children learn by hearing stories. Whether it's fairy tales like "Sleeping Beauty" and "Cinderella" that show the gentle hero living happily ever after, or darker stories that show the dangers of misbehaving.

Reading to your children is a wonderful way to teach them the power and pleasure of being read to and teaching them to want to read.

But making up stories for your children, including them in the stories as a brave knight or a fair princess, can teach children the power of imagination . . . and can be a wonderful way to get them to sit still and be quiet for a little while!

Reading old books and fairy tales can also be a great way for you, as a parent, to connect with your own childhood. What a rewarding experience it can be to get reacquainted with that old book that your own mother or father used to read to you, but now seeing it through your child's eyes!

Of course, as rewarding as your role of storyteller may be, there are parts of it that will make you wish you'd never even told your child about books. When you've read *Curious George* three times a night for the last two weeks, for instance, you may be tempted to "accidentally" lose the book. You read to them so they can fall asleep, but you find you fall asleep first!

You might even be tempted to change the story to entertain yourself. But look out if you do! Although they don't have any idea yet what those words are on the page, your child will know it the exact second you change even a single word of the book. As with so many other aspects of parenting, your job is to be patient and remember that it's all about your child. After all, you want the best for them, and that includes making them as happy as you can.

After all, no matter how frustrated you may sometimes get with them, they won't stay this age forever, and you will definitely miss these years (at least some of us will).

With the many hats a mother wears, it's truly never enough. What about all the unexpected ones that come up at any spur of the moment? Like a therapist, like an immediate medical faculty when your child doesn't feel well at any moment? It doesn't matter where you are, or why it happens, you just jump into action, just like a superhero or a ninja. Because you really are a superhero, or at least you pretend to be. And it is expected of you. What about a lifeguard, a waitress, a seamstress, a maid, a secretary to keep track of all your kids' appointments? The list can go on and on and on and on . . .

How do we make it happen? . . . I used to ask myself that question. We just do. . . . No matter what it takes, no thinking about it, no figuring out, no contemplating. When your kids need you, *EVERYTHING STOPS*! The world is put on hold. Do our kids realize this, or do they just realize that the job gets done?

In the process of making everything and anything happen by any moment, by the snap of a finger, by the flip of a switch, by running through flames and climbing mountains. Whatever we need to do (LOL), how can they still have the nerve to say to us, "MOM, YOU'RE SO ANNOYING!!!!"

Conclusion

Now that my children are older, I started to notice a very interesting thing happening. I've noticed that my kids are starting to do the same kind of thing that they told us that we were being so annoying about. They worry about us like they are the parent!! Telling us to be careful, be safe, wear our seatbelts, chew good so we don't choke. It's very funny, but do we tell them, "Oh my G-d, you're being so annoying"? *NEVER!*

Just the other day, when my son came home from a full day of work as an adult, my husband and I started bombarding him with questions.

"How was your day?"

"How's the new company?"

"Did you experience any new and exciting situations?"

"Did you meet a lot of new people?"

Etc., etc., etc.

I stopped for a minute and said to myself, "Wow! You really are so annoying . . ."

But seriously, the fact that they've gotten old enough to worry about their parents underlines what a rewarding job parenting is, if you do a good job and raise your kids right.

Although parents say being a parent is a job you don't get paid for, it really is the highest paying job in the world! Seeing your children grow and develop into the most caring, loving, intelligent, special, annoying moms and dads like us, is priceless and I wouldn't trade it in for anything in the world! In fact, I'd happily do it all over again.

For as many times as my kids told me how annoying I was, as I said in my book, "Mom, You're So Annoying!" I have to say my kids adore me. I must have done something right . . .

The End